BEC.

A WORD

•

Amy Chapeskie
Angel Rosen
Anita Clipston
Annassez
Ashley Plumridge
Casey Bottono
Elizabeth Hope
Estelle Olivia
Ian Colín Roditi
Jorge Silva
Kait Moon
Katy Lewellen
Vicki Gabow

Cover image by Kait Moon

Contents

.

Foreword

The writing of poetry can allow others a glimpse into our hearts and minds. It requires a sense of vulnerability and courage all at once. These poems were written with emotion in mind and a passion in our hearts for sharing our experiences with the world. We traverse emotions and continents with our words and stretch them out before you, our readers.

-    Vicki Gabow

Poems

Amy Chapeskie is a lifelong admirer of words and all that they can do.

Finally finished with grad school, she is happy to play a little more freely with her writing and let the words romp as they will.

Speaking of

When I speak to you of my love I speak it into existence
When I say the words the emotion reifies itself
With breath and the constriction of my diaphragm and
a flick of my tongue
It is so

Parentheses

I think in parenthesis (I think).
I speak in parenthesis (sometimes, always awkwardly).
I write in parenthesis (a lot) because I argue and debate
(everything).

With each sentence I long to slide them in there, long to
wrap them around my statements, as if to say: but
maybe not... just in case... but what if...

Some people have an angel and a devil on each shoulder
and I do too (kind of).
Except I have two devils, one for the prosecution and
one for the defence and they're both advocates for
whatever side is the opposite of what I've just said or
thought or felt.
They sit there in their pressed suits of tasteful shades of
grey and whisper and question and yell in my ears,
ensuring that I never miss the other side (because
maybe not... just in case... but what if...).

The devils don't want my soul they want my words (at
least, I think they do).

And so I think in parenthesis (and I write in
parenthesis) and if only I could really speak in
parenthesis then maybe the world would understand
that I'm not an idiot, not an awkward freak, that I do
know what I'm thinking about.
But, because I can't, I say the wrong thing or I say only
half of the conversation that's running in my head and I
don't understand why they don't understand (because I
don't understand).

And when I think and speak and write in parenthesis I am safe (cushioned by qualifications).

I wrap those little bent pieces around me like a scarf, like a shield, like a warm pair of lover's arms that will keep me safe, will keep me together as these voices war in my head.

I wrap them around me to say 'just - just listen, maybe I'm not sure, maybe there's other possibilities here' and that's okay and that's good (and that's better).

Because when I think and speak and write in parenthesis I am whole (because I am flexible and open).

Because what if... just in case... but maybe not...

Golden

In the glimmering golden
I see the fire of the year fading away
Igniting the world around me, it cannot stay

In the glimmering golden
I long to climb the rolling hill
To set off across the land, free to follow my own will

In the glimmering golden
The light shifts, shimmers and glows
Hidden glory shines through, inner beauty shows

In the glimmering golden
I think of the cold winds to come
Then I close my eyes and turn my face to the sun

waiting

the future lies before me
our future
a sun dappled path
with its share of shadows
and ups and down
it's all there so close and clear
and yet completely possibly
not there at all

it's all there until it isn't
two hours over coffee
will make it into reality
or into fiction
how wondrous is this life
that what is to be can exist
and not
all at the same time
the cat isn't dead
until you open the box

fuck
i wish you'd just
call already

Victory

Me on the verge.
Moving, changing, readying myself for what is to come.
Loving the now (mostly) but rushing headlong into
future nonetheless.
How can I not?
How can I wait?
Fear, excitement, joy and sorrow all jumbled together
make up the soundtrack of my heart.
Life moving on around me, with me, as I hold tight,
careening forward desperately hoping I manage to miss
the darkness.
The darkness swirls on the edges, nibbling at the
fringes, but I hold it back, my love, my life, a candle
from which it shrinks away.
I smile over the victory briefly before running on, eyes
wide and heart open.

Sunrise

They say it gets darkest just before dawn
Well then the sun should be coming up just about any
time now
The dark and cold wrap around me
Old friends, they are comforting in their familiar
presence
But even as I embrace them I turn my face to the east

And I wait

(almost) a haiku

knit it whole
bring something into the world
live what you make

Angel Rosen is a poetess, artist and legal secretary. She believes in art and asking, and uses both to spread love and listening.

Until I ate the Baby's Breath

I am Sick in my fingers and out of my mouth!
I can't open it to foul strangers
I whisper like wolf, teeth bared.
My heart sits in my throat,
I roar and it metastasizes.
I hemorrhage
my prefrontal cortex, the abuse victim of
women on the sun!
Without shoes!
In skirts of straw and satin.
Oh, God, do they burn.
My eyes used to be blue, you know.
Until I ate the baby's breath
Oh.... the innocence
Until I swallowed.
My eyes are green now, you know.
I am practically a snake!
And about just as good at climbing,

They fear my poison but the proper word
is venom and I do not bite
I enhance,
submerge, swallow
and singe, siren.

How Big of Us

The sky is full of you and me,
and I think it's rather big of us
to be too busy raining to matter
who we're watering and who we're drowning
I think it's mighty of us to stand still
and place our droplets upon the sandy
and the snowy places without asking the feet
which weather they can weather,

I don't feel so good about starving
out some flowers and letting the other ones
uproot in the storm,
stems and leaves carried down the drain as it were.
Others remain intact,
but still we stand.
Forgetting to consider anything
How we ever got to be clouds, I don't know.

Fox Moon

I fell in love with a fox
while trying to find
an animal to call my body.
I was shaped like nothing but myself
and lost in it too,
geometry failed to tell me
exactly what angle
my back is supposed to be arched at
when someone told me they loved me

I fell in love with a fox once but
foxes like that get tongue-tied
and so I spoke in a detangling voice,
I told her my favorite phase of the moon is
a waxing gibbous
and that is the phase of a fox
almost entirely there
all bright and noticed
whole enough to light your eyes in it
but still
quietly incomplete

Anita Clipston

I have worked in the arts my whole life so far in various forms and ways, but never felt like I was doing something worthwhile.

It took all my strength to walk away from a career I had worked so hard to get, but my path lies elsewhere.

My true goal would be to open a nonprofit school, where people from all walks of life could come and create art in all its forms. I would like to bring art to all those who have never had a chance to create. So many people have never had the opportunity through family, money, or life to be able to afford art.

Creation is such a powerful tool in all our lives and is healing on so many levels. Without art I know I would not be the person I am. It has saved my life literally

Moment

If love a fleeting moment in time
a soft kiss
the touch of a hand
or the raw passion of a embrace
then it is better to have this for a moment
than never at all

Reflection

is in mirror reflection
and slight distortions
revealing truth and fate
and the smallest of imperfections
once seen hard to stop
the blurring of vision

Life's Play

like leaves
our paths float and entwine
and then blow gently away
with the wind of time

Flowing

in a split second time changes
and things move on like rivers
gently flowing together
and then in different directions
on their way to joining up again
with the ocean that is life
Ever changing ever evolving

Now

sometimes time moves fast
and has no time to heal the regrets of the past
or the worry for the future
but living in the moment
heals all wounds and hearts

Love

don't give it a beginning
and a end
just let it be
what it wants to become
and see what happens

Patterns

Let the past remain in the past
the future take care of itself and live in the now
If you live by the past
you will do what you always did
and life will be what is always was
and not what it could be

Green

Like a dagger in my heart
she strikes with words
like poison apples
set to touch lips
undeservedly
unknowingly
and with one bite
truth is revealed
and fate unraveled

Washed away

The leaves move gently
light through the canopy gently touches the ground
Words written
then brushed away back into the earth
The trees taking in the knowledge gained and memories
left
till the wisdom gained flows into the leaves that touch
the sky above
Then all floats away on the gentle wind
Gone but not forgotten
until all that is left is just peace

The Veil

a silken thread
a hold on this world
barely
slight motion
moving the soul from its sleep
fighting from letting go
night falls
dew glistening
light catching the beauty
soul breathing

Dawn

The light breaks through the cracks
flowing gently
warming
bringing life
a quick movement
flooding the air
glowing
dressing the sky
with loving wings of dragonflies

Childhood Hopes

Frozen
Darkness seems to swell over me
Like ice creeping across a lake
Slowly devouring life
Frozen heart
Passion drowning
Sinking to the depths
Fighting for breath
Looking for air
In darkness hidden wrecks
Shadows of dreams lost
Pain in every broken shard
Breathing still just
No Light
No Guide
Just Frozen in time and place

Annassez

I'm a French singer and pianist and I also paint and write.

I always try to speak my truth and to be connected with my feelings.

I rarely write in English but sometimes, it happens. I love how the words sound.

Because of a word

Because of a word
A world is falling apart
But i get that
A word could kill
A word could hurt
But a word could heal
A word could build
Our world
Because of a word
We fought
But i get that
There's a world in a word
Sometimes i wish i could be a bird
Birds just sing
But birds fight too
For food or love
And love is all
Because of a word
A world is falling apart
But i get that
Maybe we could
Simply get back
And take a breathe
And take a break
And take a hand
And end the fight
Turn on the light
Right ?
Maybe we could
With a single word
Re-build our world
And love each other
Again
Maybe we could
Maybe we should

With a single word
Re-build our world
And take a breathe
All together
And love each other
Again
The only word
I'd like to tell
Is love
Cause love is all
Love is all
Love is you
Love is all

Life & Death

In about 6 hours from now
I will be in front of you
Dead
I will face you
Death
There will be only darkness
And tears
And fears
Because of you
Dead
Because of you
Death
In about 6 hours from now
I will be in front of you
Dead
In about 6 hours from now
The darkness will eat
Me
And I will stand up in front of you
Dead
So now I am just hunting the light
Light is my only weapon
For fighting you
Death
I won't let you eat me
Alive
I won't let you eat
Life
Death

It's been a while

It's been a while since
You told me all those awful words
And then left me
It's been a while since
My heart is bleeding
Your words are knives
But no one can see
Blood on the floor
Invisible i'm invisible
Suddenly this morning
The phone is ringing
It may be you so i'm running
I don't want to miss you
'Cause i miss you
But as i'm in pain since
You left me
I didn't clean the house
The floor is dirty so i'm sliding
Before having the chance to know
If it was you
If it was you
And now i'm bleeding on the floor
Like the poor thing i've always been
And now my pain is real
I'm bleeding for real
I'm not invisible anymore
And that's something
That's something
My pain is real
It's been a while since
The floor is dry
And I cleaned the blood
And didn't cry at all
And didn't cry at all
But suddenly the bell's ringing

It's happening again
I still miss you
Maybe it's you
So i'm running to the door
But as i didn't eat so much
Since you left me
My legs are shaking
And my heart is beating too fast
And i'm falling like an autumn leaf
On the fucking kitchen's floor
Then i'm dying
Like the poor thing
I've always been
But this makes me laugh
'Cause i'm feeling real
I'm finally dead
I'm really dead
My feeling's real
Now you could see
How I really feel since
You told me all those awful words
And then left like the poor thing
I've always been
Now i'm real
I'm dead for real
I'm dead for real
Look what you did to me
Words could kill
That's finally visible
I'm dying
I still miss you
But look at me
I'm finally not
Invisible
Anymore
And when the policemen
Finally found me

They're wondering
Why is she smiling ?
They're wondering
Whe is she smiling ?
And i'm whispering
Because i'm real
And i'm whispering
Yes, i was real
Your words killed me.

Ashley Plumridge is a 28 year old artist living in Indianapolis.

She enjoys comic books, painting and playing RPG video games.

Ashley struggles daily with depression, anxiety and chronic pain, all of which she expresses using various art forms.

The Rain

The clouds roll in, the field darkens.
A woman wanders alone,
Not lost but always searching.
She fears the rain, it pierces her heart.
Lightning crashes and trees split.
Sky rumbles while the ground shakes.
The woman falls to the ground,
Her black hair falling over her shoulders
The rain starts to fall.
Clutching her knees, she hopes it ends.
A crow flies overhead, it's screech echoing,
Familiar face, feathers quick.
The woman knows the end is near.
Closer and closer, louder and louder,
Over again and all at once.
The women cries out-
A final boom and then it stops.
Ahead, a wolf shows itself from across the field.
The clouds part, blue and yellow swirls.
Standing up, the woman pushes her hair from her eyes.
The wolf is there.
The woman is not alone.
There is hope.
At least for now.

The Darkest Blue Sky

The rays of the sun bounce off his shoulders
But he doesn't feel them.
He doesn't notice the blue skies
or the way the dandelions have made the earth yellow,
in rough patches here and there.

A squirrel runs up a tree,
finding his safe spot.
The robins sing peacefully and beautifully.
A tune of happiness and wanting.

All he hears is silence,
and the sound of his heart
pounding against his hollow chest.

He walks past children
dancing in a sprinkler.
They giggle as the water
gives them goosebumps.
He doesn't look up.
He doesn't care to see what is causing the smiles.

So many beautiful things in the world
to see and experience,
but he can't see them.
The darkness weighing heavy on his head and heart.
It's just about too much to bear.
He's exhausted and close to giving up.

"How can anything get better?" he says
While he is drowning and gasping for air.
Every day he is drowning.
Every day he feels the heavy darkness,
crushing his will to keep walking.

It's a dark day, as are most days,
But maybe one day... It will be brighter.
He doesn't give up.
He keeps trying.

He keeps walking, hands in his pockets.
His heart beating against his empty chest.
It's painful, but he keeps walking.
Perhaps one day he will find his safe spot.

Casey Bottono is a poet and writer interested in the line between grief and growth. Exploring this is a major theme of her work.

Arbitrary Memories

Symbolism in a small circle
Of chocolate kindness
Orange flavoured - the last was mint

Generosity and sharing
Were part of your being.
Every time - 'You want this?'
Stumped by kindness, I'd often decline

I'd forgotten all this, until last night
Another friend, another small chocolate disc
Another coffee you'll never see

Elizabeth Hope is studying to be a teacher, and makes her home in Oakland, California. She is a Hufflepuff who loves community building and pancakes, and she has recently begun exploring what it looks like to write poetry about the experience being on the autism spectrum.

"Intonation" is one of those poems.

Intonation

I have to work extra hard
for my words to be perceived as genuine
I am writhing on the pointed end
of your understanding of my twisting hands,
my halting words,
the moments it takes me to respond
because I am taking in data
from places you gloss over without a thought
and that means I take a little longer
getting to where you are.

"Couldn't you be a little warmer?"
my mother asks, listening to my voice captured on
video
with the chatter of thirteen-year-olds lapping against
the stones of my words.
"No," I want to respond, "Or at least, not that way."

Have a little patience, as I intone
the long-dormant phrases
I have heard others say,
and pile my own feelings
like pillows behind their sleepy heads,
and sooth their cramped shoulders
as they are jostled into waking.

Fire and Simplicity

(Haiku written after seeing Amanda Palmer play in Chicago, May 7, 2015)

Moon across her face
All-encompassing embrace,
none here to tear down.

Many eyes stinging,
the privilege of living
flattens air in the room.

Fire, simplicity,
peace and electricity--
This city holds me.

Estelle Olivia is a writer, artist, actress and creator of all sorts based in Brooklyn. She rarely means to write poetry but it happens all the same. Sometimes so unconsciously she'll find it later and wonder who has been scribbling in her notebooks.

3/27/13

And then comes the inevitable downfall after such a
short-lived high.
The inevitable, the hated
The slow melancholy seeping in,
The worthlessness that reclaims its rightful place in the
hallowed halls of my bones,
That settles itself back on the high seat in my ribcage
Luxuriates in my very heart as I look on
Impotent with hatred and shackled by my own hands

Untitled

If you ever remember me just send something my way
Some bit of fluff floating in the corner, I'll believe that
it's you
I want bigger and better
Depth and grandeur
All these true story ghosts call to me from lives no one
remembers
I wonder how I look from the outside in
There is an exhaustion here I can't seem to reconcile
With my supposed-to's and my should-have's
I can't hold still, can't hold on to so many commands
Desperately trying to stay awake for a life I'm barely
sure is real
I can feel it inside me, fully formed
If I could just align the transparencies so the light shines
through
I am doomed
Maybe if I stop trying good things will come
The excellence of habit
I never want to sleep, afraid of that quiet
Afraid of waking to face a new day unchanged

The Love Song

And it has been worth it, after all
Worth the heartache, worth the struggles
Worth the two ton stares
Worth putting on airs
Worth it to give in
All I'm worth
In bags and bins
Boxed away, archived over years
Never worth the tears
They were never worth the worry I gave
The love I crave
But it has been worth it, after all
Worth it to open my drawers
To brighten

Homeward

I walk,
A cigarette unfamiliar on my lips
But this is a private pleasure.
Three in the morning, there is no one to see
As I struggle to smoke with five hardcover tomes
balanced against my hip.
Each book offers a single relevant page
And their corners dig into my belly.
But the books help. They ground me.
The night is still and my body is ready for bed
Though my head is spinning.
I am still tonight. My hands are not shaking,
No knee bouncing in anticipation,
I am part of this night.
A passerby in the un-silent dark
As the ducks on the lake rustle in sleep
And call softly at my passing

Day Slows

Day slows and morning grows
Nearer to me
With places I could also be
Al the ways I could've seen
I've been slipping away
And catching back on
Not knowing what it means to regress
I haven't been able to express to myself
The thing that I'm missing
As if I've had it all my life
I can't be sure if I have ever known
The things that I say
I buy my own stories
To know what I've been
Though I can't be sure what I've had
So I don't think too hard
Don't push walls too thin
To bear my weight
Walls too thin so things squeeze through
I had never intended to know
Never intended to own

Day slows and morning grows nearer again
The sun slipping quietly by
I notice
My anticipation builds
The sooner to see blank space made full

Summer's Remembrance

There is a feeling of the air against my skin
When it brushes against me with seeming purpose
And we are both aware, the gentle swaying air and I.
It is seeking me out
It carries some memory of a future muddied with a past.
Of a future that could grow out of a past I have half
forgotten
If only I could pull those moments in, gather them
around me as I once did
As I once wrapped myself in them as a guard against the
rest of the world.
The new, bright, interesting world I had dropped into
Which lacked all the dust and antiquity
Without the vitality of life, the necessity, the urge
Those layers of trying of living, thrumming deep and
quiet under the every day chatter
And the feeling that I was a part of it all
An aspect of that city, of that country
A cog, a character
That I was meant to be,
Welcomed in by the very buildings of teak and bamboo
and cheap plaster.
The air whispers of these feelings, these memories of a
way I was
A way I was needed and included, a part of the place,
the life I was leading.
And if only I could capture that
The elusive creature of my memory
My childhood
My self
My very person, my being as I once was
Well before I was stripped down and squeezed through
to the present.
It strokes against my skin with the memory of a future
that I was going to have

Would have seized with the power of those streets,
With the backing of ancestors and history and
remembering and purpose.
I am reminded of a future that is still there, in the future
But that I no longer seem quite able to fill,
A future I have become deflated for.
I need to remember who I was
Remember it in my flesh, touched by this breeze.

Be

Be,
Stop this thinking you do, it is only destructive.
Let it wash away in the sound of keys, the scratch of
pens.
You don't yet know all the things you can be, this is
new.
Your hurt can be soothed, your infection can be
excised, can be spread.
If they want to wait you will leave them behind.
The world is here for your creation, for your
destruction.
It is here for your scrapping, your reproduction,
Your glue and your tape, any marks you may make.
There is nothing to be afraid of.
I do love you, you know, for all the pain I have caused I
love you still.

I don't know what it is I've been doing, what I'm meant
to do.
Don't know how or when I became so neurotic.
I want you to understand but even I am not sure.
I have had success in so many ways. What do people do
day to day?

I'm collecting scraps, hoping they can be fit together
into something worthwhile
Comprehensible.
But I'm always confused, don't remember what I've
already known.
I go back on myself, betray my every intention
Though I'm terrified of losing a single moment, a single
word.
I've become disjointed, and I can't pinpoint the initial
blow that threw me out of alignment
Don't know what went first.

Only that the puppetry was set askew, strings pulled by
opposing forces
And though I'm made real my limbs have never settled
in place
And I can't make sense of any of this.
Overburdened and verbose
I crave simplicity
a clear sightline
a view
All these reminders never do me any good.
I repeat myself but they don't sink in.

Unbelong, enough.

I remember when I wasn't sure that I belonged.
It was always.
But I loved it all the same, I took advantage of the
moments I could.
And god I wasn't going to stop living my life.

I've lost you now
My suspicions seem confirmed for all their fallacy.
What is the precise length of time a friendship must last
before you can feel deserving even after it ends?
Will I always take these breaks as surety that truly I am
not everything I want to be?

But then, who gives a shit?
Life can seem so large and ungraspable,
But really it is so very small. The only existence is the
moment in which you are living.
The sip, the step, the breath, the glance, the second
longer of inertia,
The wish that someone would jump through your
window and kill you all,
Just kill me now.

So on, as ever
Unbelong, as always.
There will be gelato and dark nights and the simple
pleasure of sleep.
Oh god, I wish I would just go to sleep
But sometimes I don't
And I'm never sure if it is punishment or reward.

So one more book that I've read before.
And one more check to see how long I've left till
morning
And a fantasy to get me through, a dark-time daydream

A downing of the last gulp I never even want.

Habit and hope and
Enough enough enough.

Just quiet, I know you know how
Drop the game, the resistance, we all know how this
ends.
I love you, it's ok. Someday it might actually be ok.
Sleep. Just stop.

Ian Colín Roditi

I write to get lost and then I write to find the way back.

Rain

Everyone runs when you arrive.
To seek shelter, to not drown or just to wait you go away.
They see you fall from the other side of the window, flooded by melancholy.
All your drops and claws echoes even on the most forgotten alleyways.
Most of them fear your howls of lighting.
They excite me. They make me feel alive.
I do run when you arrive, I run to the unknown, to be vulnerable before the two stars that see me between the grey clouds of your body.
They watch me.
I seek you.
The trees shout that I should run.
That I must get to a safe place.
To a dry place.
Out of your reach.
But I ran, to you.
And when our eyes met, I opened my arms, ready to be flooded.
You fell on me like a thunder and I got to the ground with just one strike.
I was a cloud and became rain with one bite.
Red.
My mother did well, naming me Rain.

Leave

Walk through a white desert, no sky and no ground.
Without destination, everything is the same wherever
you look.
If something isn't, you're beginning to imagine.

Imagine trees standing on their roots, rivers that run.
Let the words be taken by the wind.

Imagine bridges to let the stories exist, fill them.
The pictures flows like a fountain and run wild to
inhabit the whiteness
But turn to dust before reaching the ground.
They become fog and mist, erasing it all.

Walk through a white desert, no sky and no ground.
Without destination, everything is the same wherever
you look.
If something isn't, you're beginning to imagine.

Imagine path to follow.
Raise your eyes to see where they lead and
far away…

                                    …a big city awaits.

                        There, where everything happen.

                                            Run.
                                            Fast.
                            For god knows how long.

                    Hope the mist doesn't get there first.

Jorge Silva is a psychoanalyst that has loved to write since he was a kid. These are some of his childhood poems.

Red and Black

A truthful and bicolor abacus holds unstable spheres,
sprouting a vulgar saliva that traverses them.
Red black, black red, the liberal factory of dreams
spills its energies in a thousand dark nightmares.

The vagabond's raincoat sleeps over my body,
full of an emaciated fury that tries to escape my fragility.
My weakness unbalanced me when I tried to taste that
concept.

The thorn annoyingly stabs my temple,
while I try to shelter the miserable labyrinth,
that ruins the red and black path.
Has color never lost its way?

Smug red wound, you boast your black resignation,
it's time to ascend with your wings along with the knowledge,
and blind with skin and scar the souls of Red and Black.

We Who End

In your whirlwinds of arrogance I pity you,
servile birds of a thousand white feathers,
I, who know you too well.
Where are the days were being messengers was enough?
Today, your pure sight make hearts explode and
the profanity of your silence pours us into the Abyss.

You have been spoiled for enough ages,
I'm fed up with your whispers in the air and your screams in
the craters;
you have been here since the dawn of the Origin,
narcissists for loving your own beauty

In Death our essence slips away in a whisper,
leaving a sickening stench as our only legacy.
Nothing has been created that can hold us here,
nothing is truly ours.

Smiles and tears fade away from our withering face,
we end up being a cradle for worms, mattress of rotten
wood.
If we swallow some of the black soil we would be feeding of
what we were.
How could you understand that, you values of infinite
permanence?

From the most humble sprout a pillar will be born that will
survive us,
the mute stones guard a categorical supremacy over us.
Only we are like the wind in his path,
only we die every dawn.

The mirror gives us each time a atrocious spectacle,
we are never the same before him. Heraclitus was not wrong.
If we had better memory, we would feel strange about who
we were.
Who has dared to think that we truly Are?
The rest… has never been ours.

In a week

in a week
no less
my face
my eyes
became my trouble

if I am not smiling
everything breaks apart
if I look
with these eyes I posses
there is a chance
that everything will fade away

you told me once
not to hate my eyes
but everyone agrees
there is darkness on them

I wish clarity in my life
no more shadows
no more darkness
just to know exactly
where I lay my feet

I am tired of quicksand,
I am tired of clouds and smoke,
I only wish to find certainty,
to feel that this is not deeply fragile

but my face, my bored face
my look, my evil, my tired look,
everything this week
became a trouble

the man I am
just give up

Kait Moon is an artist, writer, parent and poet.
Her body of work has become a perpetual mixed and
multi-media art project.
Using paint, collage, words, video and audio to create
connection.

Brother

I know what it's like
to not know
how to feel safe.
I can't promise
that I will
be a safe place
for you,
Because
I have my own
wars raging.
But we can be
each other's shelter
while the shells fall
and I will not
let go of your hand.

Katy Lewellen hails from north Texas where she spends her time petting dogs and writing poems. Within the last ten years she has self-published three poetry books in addition to a handful of free poetry e-books.

Apples to Ashes

summer heat creeping in
English ivy/morning fog/unforgiving crow's caw
the crossword of
    find where it hurts –
    pinpoint the feeling &
    learn to detach

the heat reminds you,
terrifies you, and
chills you
slip the memory – a sieve
    yards full of weeds/apple cores/ sno-cone artificial
    you still swallow pills
    still swallow stories
    still freeze when the sun shines
        through windows and
        turns your skin that familiar shade of
        red.

Brine

honeysuckle & sea's brine
i have tasted delicate on my tongue
& daring across my lips
dancing divine

     caterwauled memories
       a train track of dissonance
       across skin and
       begging bone

summer traces shadows
strawberry & over-ripe
wavelengths into cores
    (prone to overreacting)
and i am purged of brine shells &
needlepoint holes

       filled with sun &
       the faint taste of honeysuckle
       blooming late in the year

Flightless

cold & ancient

we were pure -
a stone bird
            blue and murmuring at dusk
through winter boughs
between long & lonely breaths
sweet summer fertile
                rain
forgive me

            there you were

Vicki Gabow is a high school English teacher by day and storyteller and poet by night. In her spare time, she enjoys communing with nature, birdwatching, making glorious messes, and crocheting. She lives in Lancaster, Pennsylvania with her husband, Dan, and two cats, Zoey, and Doodle.

Remembrance and Longing

Watching sunlight's glimmer in the rear view mirror
as I pass beneath the shadowed canopy of maple, oak,
and birch -shimmering slivers of light
reflecting and refracting as it filters through.
In the moment it brings joy, but looking back
I long for more.

The road I know so well
leading straight to heart and home; they come
to represent it in my dreams –
shaking off the dusty covers as I sleep.
The cobwebs disappear and I am transported
though dreams distort and warp and people and things
are not where they were left.

Morning fog, too, waxes nostalgic in autumn for
days which can't return,
tucked carefully away in memory. The sweet
smell of decaying leaves and freshly opened crayons
catches in my throat and forces a sigh
at once bitter and sweet.

Places once forgot
exist still in the sleeping mind
bringing forth new actors to the stage.
Events and people mix at awkward intervals
as though editing the reel of time.

Some say dreams allow us to
resolve inner turmoil in sleep that in waking
hours can't be done. Sometimes it seems
they remind us what's worth remembering
of our patchwork quilted days.

Sometimes they refuse our right to forget how it
really was when emotions were so fresh and raw
reopening scars once healed.

Remembrance and longing, which one leads
and which one follows the other
out the door?

Natural Disasters

Emotions are such fickle things
        they change direction like the wind
     as a new front blows
        through the upper atmosphere.
               The whirl-wind tour
just a twister in the night
       sneaking in with stealth surprise
     catching us off guard;
   wrecking hearts, upending homes, hurtling lives into
          chaos.
These emotions can be tricky
      at best, and down right
                  messy and
         destructive in the darkest skies.
All thunderbolts and lightning
        howling winds and cries.

This earthquake shakes me from my foundation firm;
    I fail to compromise. Without that give and take,
          this house will surely crumble.
The once tall tree lies now
        upon it's side, roots exposed and
raw.
      Nothing is safe from the avalanche of emotions;
tears crashing down mix with mud and stones that
anger throws.

No shelter or comfort from our own hurricane eyes,
   what damage we might wreak upon our own shores
       as high as the tides might rise.
We can be sun, ice, snow, wind, and rain
      all with in a day,
          or even hour.

These emotions hold disproportional power;
they are grand forces of nature
with which we cannot reckon.
Humans capable of thought and feeling are just natural
disasters.

Contact Information of the Poets

Amy Chapeskie
chapeskie@gmail.com

Angel Rosen
poisonedforlife@gmail.com

Anita Clipston
therestlesscreative@gmail.com

Annassez
annaellee@gmail.com
www.patreon.com/annassez

Ashley Plumridge
emotionalshenanigans@gmail.com

Casey Bottono
www.caseybottono.com
shadywilbury@gmail.com

Elizabeth Hope
www.verbalpowers.tumblr.com
lizhpowers@gmail.com

Estelle Olivia
estelle.olivia@gmail.com

Ian Colín Roditi
wordbending@gmail.com
www.QuinqueStories.net
www.Patreon.com/QuinqueStories

Jorge Silva
jorge.silva.rodighiero@gmail.com
www.soyjorgesilva.com

Kait Moon
www.kaitmoonarts.com
www.patreon.com/kaitmoon

Katy Lewellen
https://www.facebook.com/Poetry-by-K-Lewellen-191378540924019

Vicki Gabow
https://vgabes42.wordpress.com/
www.twitter.com/ vgabes42
https://www.facebook.com/dabbleandpluck/

32225832R00051

Made in the USA
Middletown, DE
27 May 2016